JUST ANOTHER COOKBOOK

VOLUME 1

APPETIZERS

Dedicated to:
My Wife Tabitha
To Whom I Hold Very
Dear In My Heart

TABLE OF CONTENTS

TABLE OF CONTENTS CONTINUED

TABLE OF CONTENTS CONTINUED

ANTIPASTO SALAD

1 lg. head lettuce, cut into 8 wedges
2 stalks fennel, trimmed & quartered
1 (6 oz.) can ripe olives, drained
1 cucumber, peeled, scored & sliced thin
1/4 lb. thin slices provolone cheese
1/4 lb. thin slices salami
1 (2 oz.) can rolled anchovy fillets

Arrange ingredients attractively on a large platter or on a lazy susan. Serve with cruets of oil and wine vinegar. An antipasto salad usually contains at least six or seven different items. Any of the following may be substituted for those already listed:

Thin slices prosciutto ham
Dry pork sausage or pepperoni
Artichoke or celery hearts
Ham slivers
Sliced or quartered hard cooked eggs
Pickled mushrooms
Peppers
Beets
Pimiento strips
Tomato sections
Green pepper rings
Green olives
Scallions
Radishes

APPETIZER MEAT BALLS

2 lbs. hamburger
1 lb. bulk pork sausage
1/2 can (5 oz.) evaporated milk
2 c. oatmeal
1/2 tsp. pepper
2 tsp. chili powder
1/2 tsp. garlic powder
2 tsp. salt
2 eggs
1/2 c. chopped onion

SAUCE:

3 c. catsup
2 1/4 c. brown sugar
1 tbsp. liquid smoke, if you like
1 tsp. garlic powder
1 c. finely chopped onions

Mix and shape into balls. Place in a 9x13 glass pan in single layer. Pour on sauce and bake 1 hour at 350 degrees.

APPETIZER SHRIMP KABOBS

2 lb. shrimp
1/2 c. lemon juice
1/2 c. vegetable oil
1/4 c. soy sauce
3 tbsp. fresh parsley
2 tbsp. chopped onion
1/2 tsp. salt
1/2 tsp. pepper
1 clove garlic, minced

Mix all ingredients together. Marinate 2 to 3 hours. Thread shrimp on wooden skewers. Broil 3-4 minutes, 6 inches from heat, on each side. Baste occasionally with reserved marinade.

APPLE - NUT - CHEESE GREEN SALAD

1/2 c. granulated sugar
1 tsp. dry mustard
1 tsp. salt
1 tbsp. minced onion
1/3 c. red wine vinegar
1 c. salad oil
1 1/2 tbsp. poppy seeds

SALAD:

Mixed crisp salad greens (spinach, leaf, and Iceberg is a good combination)
Crisp apple cubes
Cashew nuts
Cubes of cheese (Havarti, Muenster, Mozzarella, or Swiss)

DRESSING:

In blender or food processor, combine sugar, mustard, salt, onion, and vinegar; blend thoroughly. Add salad oil and poppy seeds and mix slightly. Chill.

Salad: Combine salad greens, apple cubes, nuts, and cheese cubes in large bowl. Toss with the dressing and serve immediately.

Note: This dressing is best used in small quantities to enhance rather than overpower the salad ingredients. This salad is also great in the summer with strips of grilled chicken breasts on top.

BACON AND WATER CHESTNUT APPETIZERS

3 cans whole water chestnuts, drained
1 lb. bacon, cut into thirds
1 1/2 c. catsup
1 1/2 c. brown sugar

Wrap bacon around chestnuts and secure with toothpicks. Bake at 350 degrees uncovered for 45 minutes. Drain.

Combine sugar and catsup to make sauce. Pour over appetizers. Bake at 350 degrees covered for another 45 minutes.

Can also be cooked in the microwave to save time.

BACON-CHEESE APPETIZERS

2 slices crisp bacon, crumbled
4 pimiento-stuffed green olives, minced
2 tsp. minced onion
1/2 tsp. seeded and minced chili pepper or 1/8 tsp. crushed red pepper
12 melba rounds

In small mixing bowl combine all ingredients except melba rounds. Onto each melba round spoon an equal amount of cheese mixture. Arrange melba rounds on nonstick baking sheet and broil until cheese is melted, about 30 seconds.

Makes 2 servings, 6 appetizers each.

BAKED POTATO SKINS

1/2 c. butter
2 garlic cloves, pressed or minced
Skins from 8 lg. baking potatoes
Freshly ground black pepper & salt to taste
1/2 c. grated Swiss cheese

Melt the 1/2 cup butter over medium heat. When the butter is hot and bubbling, add the garlic. Saute the garlic until softened and fragrant (about 2 1/5 minutes). Cut each potato skin in half lengthwise into 2 equal pieces. Brush the bottom and interior of each piece with the garlic butter. Place each piece, scooped side up, on a shallow baking sheet. Sprinkle generously with ground pepper. Sprinkle lightly with salt to taste. Scatter the grated cheese lightly on top of the buttered skins. Preheat oven to 350 degrees. Place the cookie sheet in the upper third of the oven. Bake the skins for 30-45 minutes or until hot, crisp and golden.

BAKED STUFFED MUSHROOMS

1 stick butter
1 small onion, minced
3 tablespoons Parmesan cheese
1/3 cup sweet Vermouth
1/2 teaspoons Worcestershire sauce
1 cup plain bread crumbs
1 lb. mushrooms (remove stems and finely chop)
1/2 teaspoon salt
1/4 teaspoon pepper
3/4 teaspoon garlic powder
1/4 teaspoon oregano

Melt butter in skillet. Cook onion until translucent. Add chopped stems. Sitr in bread crumbs, seasonings, and cheese. Brown lightly. Add sweet Vermouth last. Toss lightly to combine well. Stuff mushroom caps with mixture. Bake at 350°F for 15 minutes.

BEAN TACO

2 Wheat flour or corn tortillas

Refried beans, heated
Salsa
Sliced black olives
Sliced green onions
Chopped tomatoes

Lightly brown tortillas in a 400 degree oven on both sides. Top tortillas with remaining ingredients in the order listed (tomatoes may either be added after or baked with other ingredients).

BEEF EGGPLANT SCALLOP

1 medium eggplant, cut into 1 - 1 1/2 inch cubes
1 lb ground beef
1/2 cup sliced onion
1 teaspoon basil, minced
2 cloves garlic, minced
2 tablespoons butter
1 can (10 3/4 oz.) Cream of Mushroom soup
1/2 cup water
1/4 teaspoon salt
1/2 cup Pepperidge Farm Herb Seasoned Stuffing
1/4 cup Grated Parmesan cheese
Hungarian paprika, for sprinkling

Cook eggplant in boiling salted water for 10 minutes. Drain and place in a 10x5x2 inch baking dish.

In a saucepan, brown ground beef, onion, and basil in butter until onion is tender and beef takes on color; add garlic half way through and do not allow to brown (remove to edges if necessary).

Stir in soup, water and salt. Pour mixture over eggplant, sprinkle with stuffing and cheese. Sprinkle top with paprika down the center.

Bake at 350°F for 30 minutes.

4-6 servings.

BEEF OR CHICKEN CHIMICHANGAS

1 lb. ground beef, browned and drained or 2 c. chicken, diced
1 c. cheddar cheese, shredded
1/2 c. onions, chopped
Salsa
2 c. lettuce, shredded
Unbaked tortillas

Spoon about 1/3 cup filling down center of each tortilla. Top each with about 2 tablespoon cheese. Fold in the 2 sides envelope fashion. Roll up each tortilla, starting from one of the short sides. Secure with wooden toothpicks.

Fry filled tortillas in a deep heavy skillet about 1 minute on each side or until crisp and golden brown. Drain on paper towels. Keep warm in a 300 degree oven while frying remaining ones. Remove toothpicks. Serve on lettuce mixture with salsa, sour cream, and/or guacamole dip.

BLUE CHEESE CRISPS

Flaky pastry sandwiches with a blue cheese filling are an easy to prepare appetizer that is sure to please guests. If you wish, you can complete the crisps ahead of time, except for the baking and freeze to store.

For 48 Appetizers You Will Need:

4 oz. blue cheese
2 tsp. instant minced onion
2 tbsp. butter
1 egg
1 (3 oz.) pkg. cream cheese
2 c. all purpose flour
1 tsp. salt
3/4 c. vegetable shortening
1/3 - 1/2 c. ice water
Grated cheddar cheese (opt.)
Paprika (opt.)

1. Beat blue cheese, onion, butter, egg and cream cheese until light and fluffy. Cover and refrigerate.

2. Measure flour and salt into mixing bowl. Cut in shortening until in pea sized particles. Sprinkle with ice water. Toss with fork until dough holds together in a ball. Divide into 2 parts.

3. Roll out pastry, one part at a time, to form a rectangle about 12"x8". Spread half the filling over half the pastry. Fold dough over to make a rectangle about 4"x12". Seal edges well. Press out air bubbles.

4. Using a pastry wheel, cut into 1" squares. Place squares on ungreased baking sheet. Sprinkle lightly with cheese and paprika if desired.

5. Repeat process with second half of pastry and filling. (Any leftover filling can be frozen for future use.

6. Bake at 425 degrees for 12 to 15 minutes or until lightly browned and puffy.

TIPS: These crispy little appetizers are pretty if you use crinkle-type pastry cutter to cut the squares. To make ahead, freeze unbaked squares in a single layer well wrapped. Bake from frozen state when ready to serve.

BLUE CHEESE SALAD DRESSING

1 c. mayonnaise or salad dressing
1 sm. onion, cut up
1/3 c. salad oil
1/4 c. catsup
2 tbsp. sugar
2 tbsp. vinegar
1 tsp. prepared mustard
1/2 tsp. paprika
1/4 tsp. celery seed
1 c. crumbled blue cheese

In blender container combine mayonnaise or salad dressing, onion, salad oil, catsup, sugar, vinegar, mustard, paprika, celery seed, 1/2 teaspoon salt and dash of pepper. Cover and blend until smooth. Transfer dressing to storage container; stir in blue cheese. Cover and chill. Makes 2 1/2 cups.

BROCCOLI CHEESE SALAD

1/2 c. salad dressing
1/4 c. sugar
1 tbsp. vinegar
Chopped broccoli tips
Shredded Cheddar cheese
1 onion, chopped

Mix sugar, salad dressing and vinegar in a small bowl. Mix in another bowl broccoli tips, cheese and onion. Combine all together and serve.

BROWN RICE CASSEROLE

1 c. raw brown rice
1 c. canned tomatoes
1/4 c. chopped onions
1 sm. garlic, grated
1/2 c. grated cheese (Parmesan)
1/4 c. olive oil
1/4 c. chopped black olives
1/4 c. sliced stuffed olives
1/4 c. chopped green peppers
4 oz. mushrooms
2 c. boiling water

Mix ingredients in casserole. Bake, covered, at 350 degrees for 1 1/2 hours.

BRUSCHETTA OF RICOTTA CHEESE WITH OLIVES

Italian bread, diagonally cut 1 inch slices
prosciutto, 3-4 thin slices
1/4 cup Calamata olives, pitted and chopped
1/2 16oz can diced tomatoes
1/4 cup onion, finely diced
1/2 Tbsp garlic, finely minced
2 Tbsp extra virgin olive oil
1/4 cup fresh parsley, finely chopped
1/2 tsp basil
1/4 tsp oregano
1 Tbsp bread crumbs
salt and pepper
1/3 cup Ricotta Cheese

Preheat oven to 425°F.

Toast bread slices for 4-5 minutes or until lightly browned.

Combine remaining ingredients in bowl and season to taste with salt and pepper.

Spoon 1 tablespoon of the tomato mixture onto each toasted slice of bread.

Roll slices of prosciutto and slice into 1/8" inch pieces. Place on top of tomato mixture and serve.

BUFFALO WING DIP

1 package softened cream cheese
2 cups cooked chunked boneless skinless chicken breast
chunky bleu cheese dressing
hot wing sauce
1 package shredded Monterey Jack cheese

Spread cream cheese in bottom of a 9x13 baking dish. Mix hot wing sauce with the chicken and pour on top of the cream cheese, spread the chunky bleu cheese dressing over chicken mixture and top with Monterey Jack cheese.

Bake until cheese is melted and bubbly.

Serve with your favorite crackers or chips. Great for football snacks!

BUFFALO WINGS

1 dozen wing pieces, thawed
oil for frying
3 tbs smart balance spread
1 1/2 tsp "i can't believe it's not butter!"
3-5 tbs hot sauce
1 tbs white vinegar
salt
pepper
bleu cheese dressing
celery sticks

Pour oil in large (12") skillet to 1" deep Heat over medium high until wooden spoon handle sizzles within 3 seconds when dipped in the oil. Fry wing pieces 15 minutes, turning a couple of times. Don't crowd the wings.

Meanwhile, add remaining ingredients to another large skillet and turn heat to low.

When wings are ready, turn up heat on other skillet to medium. Remove each wing piece with tongs and shake off excess oil, drop into other skillet. Shake skillet frequently to coat wings in sauce, for 3-5 minutes, until wings are browned.

Remove to plate, serve with celery and bleu cheese dressng.

Serves 1-2

CANNELLONI

2 c. tomato sauce
2 c. bechamel sauce
1/2 c. Parmesan cheese (1/4 c. for finishing, 1/4 c. for stuffing)
12 cooked fresh pasta rectangles, about 3 1/2 x 4 1/2 inches
The stuffing

INGREDIENTS FOR STUFFING:

1/2 lb. veal, ground
1/4 lb. mushrooms, chopped
1 onion, chopped
2 cloves garlic, minced
1/2 tsp. dried oregano
1/2 tsp. dried basil
1/2 tsp. dried thyme
1/2 tsp. dried rosemary
2 tbsp. tomato paste
1/4 c. Parmesan cheese
1/2 lb. ricotta cheese
1 pkg. fresh spinach, cooked and chopped fine

Use 2 teaspoons each if fresh.

Saute veal in a little oil until it changes color. Remove from pan. In a little more oil, saute the onion until transparent. Add the garlic, herbs and mushrooms. Cook over low heat for 3 minutes or until the herbs become fragrant. Add the tomato paste and cooked veal. Mix well. Then add the Parmesan cheese. Let cool slightly. Add the chopped spinach and ricotta cheese to the veal. Season to taste with salt, pepper and nutmeg.

Arrange the rectangles of pasta, flat. Place a line of filling on each and roll into tube shapes. In the bottom of a baking dish, place the tomato sauce. Arrange the cannelloni on top in one layer. Top with bechamel sauce and Parmesan cheese. Bake at 350 degrees for 20 minutes or until hot and the cheese is browned. Serve with a mixed green salad and Italian wine. Serves 4.

CHEESE CANAPES APPETIZER

1/2 lb. shredded cheddar cheese
1/2 lb. fried crisp bacon
2 tsp. Worcestershire sauce
1 tbsp. minced onion
1/4 tsp. pepper
1 c. mayonnaise

Cut crust off white sandwich bread (Pepperidge Farm type). Spread mixture on bread, cut in quarters. Bake at 450 degrees for 8 to 10 minutes.

CHEESE MOLD

2 (3 oz.) pkgs. cream cheese
1/2 tsp. Worcestershire sauce
1/4 tsp. salt
Garlic powder, to taste
1/2 tsp. chili powder
1 tsp. curry powder
1 c. pecans, finely chopped
Lemon juice

Blend all ingredients together very well. Pour into mold and chill in the refrigerator overnight. Wash and slice apples to make wedges and dip into lemon juice and water to preserve color. Unmold cheese and surround with sliced apples.

CHEESE PUFFS

1 (4 oz.) container whipped cream cheese
1 egg
1 tsp. lemon juice
1 tsp. frozen chives
1/2 c. (2 oz.) shredded sharp white natural cheddar cheese
4 slices bacon, crisp-cooked, drained & crumbled
4 frozen patty shells, thawed

Combine cream cheese, egg, lemon juice, chives and a dash of pepper; beat well. Stir in cheddar cheese and bacon. Chill. Roll 1 of the patty shells to 8 x 4 inch rectangle. Cut into 2-inch squares. Top each square with a rounded teaspoon of filling. Brush edges with milk. Fold to form triangle; seal. Place on ungreased baking sheet. Repeat with remaining shells and filling. Chill appetizers until ready to bake. Place in 450 degree oven. Immediately reduce temperature to 400 degrees, bake 12 to 15 minutes. Makes 32 appetizers.

CHEX PARTY MIX

1/2 c. butter
1 1/4 tsp. seasoned salt
4 1/2 tsp. Worcestershire sauce
2 c. Corn Chex
2 c. Rice Chex
2 c. Bran Chex
2 c. Wheat Chex
1 c. salted mixed nuts

Heat butter in large shallow roasting pan. Stir in seasoning; add Chex and nuts. Mix until all pieces are coated. Heat 1 hour at 250 degrees. Stir every 15 minutes. Makes 9 cups. May be frozen; thaw at room temperature in container in which it was stored.

CHICKEN AND VEGETABLE EGG ROLLS

1/2 cup dried mushrooms
1 each chicken breast, skin, split
1 each clove garlic, minced
1 tablespoon oil
1 can 16-oz bean sprouts, drained
2 cup small spinach leaves
1/2 cup green onion thin sliced
1/2 cup bamboo shoots, thin sliced
2 tablespoons soy sauce
2 teaspoons cornstarch
1 teaspoon grated ginger root
1 teaspoon sugar
1/4 teaspoon salt
12 each egg roll skins
oil for deep-fat frying

Soak mushrooms in warm water for 30 minutes; drain and chop, discarding stems.

Chop chicken for filling. Stir-fry chicken and garlic quickly in 1 T hot oil about 2 minutes.

Add vegetables, stir-fry about 3 minutes more.

Blend soy sauce into cornstarch; stir in ginger root, sugar and salt.

Stir into chicken minture; cook and stir until thickened. Cool.

Place egg roll skin with one point toward you. Spoon 1/4 cup filling diagonally across and just below center of skin.

Fold bottom point of skin over filling; tuck point under filling.

Fold side corners over, forming an envelope shape. Roll up.

Fry egg rolls, a few at a time, in deep hot oil (365 degrees) for 2-3 minutes or until golden brown.

Drain on paper towels.

CHICKEN CHILI NACHOS

4 chicken breasts, boiled and shredded
2-8 oz packages of cheese (cheddar, jack, Colby)
1 or 2 cans spicy chili beans
16 oz. sour cream
1 can of cream of chicken soup
1 can of diced tomatoes with green chilies
1 small can diced chilies or jalapenos
1-2 bags of nacho cheese Doritos

In large pot add sour cream, soup, tomatoes, chilies, and chicken. Let simmer 10-15 minutes. Layer baking dish with smashed Doritos, then pour chicken mixture on top.

Next spread half an 8 oz. package of cheese, then add cans of beans, and top with remainder of cheese.

Bake at 350 degrees for 20-30 minutes until cheese is melted.

Serve with additional Doritos instead of a fork.

CHICKEN MAZZETTI

1 lb. onion, diced
1 1/2 c. green pepper, diced
1 1/2 c. celery, diced
1 clove garlic, minced
2 (6 oz.) cans tomato paste
3 (8 oz.) cans tomato sauce
1 (10 oz.) can Campbells tomato soup
1 (12 oz.) bottle stuffed green olives with juice
Paprika
1 (8 oz.) can mushrooms, stems & pieces
1 (3 oz.) can sliced ripe olives
2 (5 oz.) pkgs. wide egg noodles
5 lbs. chicken (breasts & thighs)
1 1/2 lbs. grated cheddar cheese
1 (4 oz.) can Parmesan cheese
1 lb. natural Mozzarella cheese
1 tbsp. Accent

Combine onion, green pepper, celery, garlic, tomato paste, tomato sauce and tomato soup in saucepan and simmer until vegetables are tender. Cook chicken in water to cover, salted to taste with Accent added, until chicken is done, about 25 minutes. Remove chicken to cool and add noodles to chicken broth. Cook noodles 7 minutes and remove from heat leaving noodles in broth until ready to use. Cut chicken from bone and cube it (about 1/2" cubes) and add to tomato mixture with Parmesan cheese and cheddar cheese (reserve some grated cheese for top). Then add mushrooms and olives. Alternate layers of drained noodles and chicken tomato mixture in wide deep casserole or baking dish. Top with reserved grated cheddar cheese and sprinkle with cubes of Mozzarella. Decorate with splotches of paprika. Bake at 300 degrees for 1 hour.

CHICKEN NACHO DIP

4 large cans white chunk chicken breast, drained
1 package cream cheese
3/4 large container of sour cream
1/2 cup salsa
1 small bottle of Ortega Taco Sauce
1 8 oz bag of shredded taco or Colby cheese
pinch of hot cayenne pepper and garlic powder (optional)
nacho chips

Preheat oven to 375F.

Combine chicken, cream cheese, and sour cream in bowl. Spread mixture in an 8X12 inch baking pan. Sprinkle lightly with a pinch of hot pepper and garlic powder, if desired.

Pour salsa and Ortega sauce over chicken mixture and top with cheese.

Bake in oven until cheese is melted. Serve warm or cold with nacho chips.

CHICKEN PARMIGIANA

1 chicken (3 lb.), cut into serving pieces
Salt to taste
Freshly ground pepper to taste
1/4 c. butter or olive oil
1 c. mushrooms, sliced
1 green pepper, cored, seeded and finely chopped
1/2 c. onion, finely chopped
1 garlic clove, finely minced
2 c. tomatoes, peeled, seeded and chopped
1/2 c. dry vermouth
1/2 c. stuffed olives, sliced
1/4 c. Parmesan cheese, grated

Sprinkle chicken with salt and pepper and brown on all sides in butter or oil in a heavy skillet. Sprinkle with the mushrooms and cook for 5 minutes. Add green pepper, onion, garlic, tomatoes and vermouth. Cover tightly and bake for 30 minutes at 350 degrees. Add olives and cook for 10 minutes longer. Serve with grated cheese. Serves 4.

CHICKEN QUESADILLAS

12 ounces cooked chicken breast halves
2/3 cup shredded monterey jack cheese
1/4 cup finely chopped green onion
8 (8") flour tortillas
1 cup salsa
1 cup sour cream

Combine chicken and salsa in bowl. Divide chicken mixture, cheese and green onions evenly among 4 tortillas.

Cover with remaining tortillas. Heat one tortilla stack in large skillet over medium heat for 2-3 minutes.

Turn tortilla over and repeat for another 2-3 minutes or until cheese is melted. Repeat with remaining tortilla stacks.

Serve with sour cream.

CHILI CHEESE CASSEROLE

1 lb. cooked, crumbled hamburg, fat drained
1 can drained kidney beans
3-4 c. cooked rice
1 lg. onion, chopped
Nacho cheese dip or spread
Louisiana hot sauce
1 pkg. taco seasoning
Salt, pepper, garlic

Combine all ingredients EXCEPT cheese in casserole dish. Smear cheese on top. Cover and bake for 30-40 minutes or until heated through. Serve with a green salad. Serves 4-6. Note: Or microwave on high for 8-10 minutes without cheese. Add cheese and microwave on high for 2 minutes. Let stand for 5 minutes.

CLAM-CHEESE DIP

1 (10 1/2 oz.) can minced clams
8 oz. cream cheese
1/2 tsp. onion salt
1 tsp. Worcestershire
Few drops of hot pepper sauce
Few sprigs parsley, chopped
Juice of 1/2 lemon

Drain clams, reserving liquid. Beat together 1/4 cup liquid, clams and remaining ingredients. Serve as dip for potato chips or crisp crackers. Makes 2 cups.

CLAMS CASINO

24 clams on the half shell (oysters & mussels may be substituted)
Lemon juice
1 1/2 c. minced green pepper
Bacon, chopped in 1" squares
Salt & pepper to taste

Over each clam, sprinkle a few drops of lemon juice, 1 teaspoon of green pepper, and a square of bacon. Sprinkle with pepper and salt. Bake in a 400 degree oven for 10-12 minutes or place under broiler for 5 minutes. Serves 8.

COCKTAIL SAUCE

1 c. ketchup
1 tbsp. horseradish
Dash of pepper
1 tsp. Worcestershire sauce
1/2 tsp. chili powder

Mix all ingredients and enjoy with seafood.

COCKTAIL SMOKIES

1 pound cocktail smokies sausages
6 ounces grape jelly
6 ounces mustard

Put all ingredients into crock pot. Sir all ingredients together as jelly melts. Simmer for 1 hour. Serve warm.

Serving Size: 12.

COTTAGE CHEESE SALAD

1 box Jello (any flavor)
1 16 oz. small curd cottage cheese
1 12 oz. can of crushed pineapple
1 10 oz. tub of whipping cream

Drain the pineapple. Mix the cottage cheese and whipping cream together, until well blended. Next, stir in the pineapple. Mix well.

Stir in Jello mix. Mix well until Jello is completely dissolved. Chill 4 hours prior to serving.

COTTAGE CHEESE VEGGIE DIP

1/3 c. milk
1 pt. cottage cheese
1/2 pkg. onion soup mix or vegetable soup mix
Lots of raw veggies, cut up for dipping

Blend 1/3 cup milk, 1 pint cottage cheese and soup mix in a bowl.

Put in refrigerator for 1/2 hour.

Serve with raw veggies. Dip and enjoy.

CRAB MEAT APPETIZER

1 (8 oz.) pkg. cream cheese
1 tbsp. milk
1 green onion, minced
1/2 tbsp. lemon juice
1 tbsp. Worcestershire sauce
1 (6 oz.) can crabmeat, drained and rinsed
1/2 c. chili sauce
Parsley or chives

Soften cream cheese. Add milk to cream cheese. Add green onion, lemon juice and Worcestershire sauce to cream cheese-milk mixture. Mound on serving plate.

Spread flaked crabmeat over mound. This may be liquid, place paper towels all around mound to absorb liquid. Chill for several hours. Remove paper towels. Pour chili sauce over mound. Garnish with parsley or chives. Surround with assorted crackers.

CRAB MEAT - BACON ROLL

1/4 c. tomato juice
1 egg, well beaten
6 1/2 to 7 1/2 pkg. crab meat, drained and flaked
1/2 c. dry bread crumbs
1 tbsp. chopped parsley
1 tbsp. lemon juice
1/4 tsp. salt
1/4 tsp. Worcestershire sauce
Dash of pepper
9 slices of bacon, cut in half

Mix tomato juice and egg. Add crab, crumbs, parsley, lemon juice, and seasonings. Mix thoroughly. Roll into 18 fingers about 2 inches long. Wrap each roll with 1/2 slice of bacon. Fasten with toothpick. Broil 5 inches from heat for about 10 minutes. Turn often to brown evenly. Enjoy!

CRABMEAT QUESADILLAS WITH TOMATILLO SAUCE

1 lb. crabmeat
1 sm. onion, finely chopped
2 cloves garlic
1 red bell pepper, chopped
1 jalapeno, seeded and chopped
1/2 c. fresh cilantro, chopped
6 oz. shredded Monterey Jack cheese
Some melted butter
Salt and pepper
12 flour tortillas

Saute the onion, garlic, red bell pepper and jalapeno pepper in butter until translucent. Add crabmeat and cilantro and adjust seasoning with salt and pepper to taste.

Soften the tortillas in a skillet. Spread some crabmeat mixture over half of the tortilla and top with Monterey Jack cheese. Fold top over. Continue until all quesadillas are assembled. Brush with melted butter. Heat a skillet over medium heat and saute the quesadillas until brown on both sides. Cut into 3 pieces and serve with tomatillo sauce.

CRAB SALAD

2 pkgs. unflavored gelatin
1/4 c. cold water
1 can tomato soup
1 (8 oz.) pkg. cream cheese, riced
1 cucumber, minced
1 tsp. grated onion
1 lg. stalk celery
4 c. crabmeat
1 tsp. salt
Dash cayenne pepper
1 c. mayonnaise

THOUSAND ISLAND DRESSING:

1 c. mayonnaise
1/3 c. chili sauce
1 tbsp. chopped chives
1 tbsp. chopped pimientos
1/2 c. whipped cream or sour cream

Combine all ingredients for dressing; serve with mold.

Soak gelatin in cold water; bring soup to a boil and dissolve the gelatin in it. Then mix with cream cheese. Combine minced vegetables with gelatin mixture. Add crabmeat (checking first for shells) and seasonings; pour into an oiled mold. Chill until firm. Unmold onto lettuce leaves and garnish with stuffed eggs and marinated vegetables. Serve with Thousand Island Dressing. Serves 8.

CRAB STUFFED MUSHROOM CAPS

24 large mushrooms
1/4 cup extra virgin olive oil
minced garlic
any flavor Philadelphia (whipped) cream cheese
1 can crab meat
Parmesan cheese
6 tablespoons butter

Remove stems from the mushrooms. Carefully trim the mushroom cap back to expose the spore area. Do this at an angle so that the cap can hold more mixture.

In a bowl, combine the container of whipped cream cheese, three tablespoons of Parmesan cheese and the crab meat. Fold the mixture over until thoroughly combined.

Pour 1/2 teaspoon of extra virgin olive oil into each mushroom cap. Add a sprinkle of minced garlic into the oil. Add one tablespoon of crab mixture into each mushroom cap. Put the mushroom caps into a foil container.

Slice the butter into cubes and add them to the bottom of the container. Sprinkle minced garlic over butter.

Cover the container with foil and bake at 350°F for 45 minutes. Switch the oven to broil and remove the foil during the last 5 minutes of cook time.

Makes 12 servings.

CREAMY ONION DIP

Sour cream
Onion soup mix
2 oz. Bleu cheese
Chopped walnuts

Blend 1 1/2 cups dairy sour cream and 2 tablespoons onion soup mix. Stir in 2 ounces Bleu cheese (crumbled) and 1/3 cup chopped walnuts. Makes about 2 cups. Serve with potato chips and pretzels.

CREOLE SHRIMP COCKTAIL SAUCE

juice of half a lemon
1 c. tomato juice
2 T. Worcestershire sauce
1 T. pepper sauce
1/2 c. celery, finely chopped
2 T. horseradish, grated

Combine all ingredients and serve over shrimp in cocktail glasses.

Serve with crisp crackers and lettuce salad if desired.

DEVILED EGGS

12 eggs, hard-boiled
1 cup Miracle Whip Salad Dressing
1 teaspoon prepared mustard, optional
1/4 cup sweet pickle relish
1 teaspoon salt

Cut eggs in half and remove the yolks. Mash with a fork then add the rest of the ingredients. Mix should be slightly moist. Spoon about 1-2 tablespoons of the filling into the egg whites or use a pastry bag to pipe the filling into the whites. Sprinkle with paprika, if desired. Cover and chill for at least one hour.

Serving Size: 24.

EASY CRAB DIP

1 package crabmeat
2 tablespoons of Miracle Whip
1 package Phildelphia cream cheese
diced onion to taste (about 1/4 of one)
1/2 stalk celery (optional)
dash salt and pepper

Blend together and enjoy.

Serve with Baquette, crackers or nacho chips.

EASY NACHOS

4-5 cups tortilla chips
1 16-ounce can refried beans
1 cup chile con queso dip
1/4 cup sliced green onions
1/2 cup sour cream
2 cups shredded iceburg lettuce
1/2 tsp freshly chopped cilantro (optional)
1 Tbs hot sauce (optional)

Warm the chile con queso dip and refried beans.

Spread the warm beans out over the chips on a serving platter. Optionally sprinkle hot sauce over the beans.

Pour on the dip, cover with shredded lettuce, a daub of sour cream, and top with green onions and a sprinkle of cilantro.

ENCHILADA CASSEROLE

2 lbs. ground beef
1 onion
1 pkg. taco seasoning
1 sm. can bean dip
1 lb. grated cheese
16 corn tortillas
Salt and pepper to taste
1 (8 oz.) can tomato juice

Brown meat and onions; drain off excess fat. Add taco seasonings and water according to directions on package. Add bean dip and then in casserole dish. Layer meat mixture, tortillas, then cheese, ending with cheese on top. Cover and bake 30 minutes at 350 degrees. Serves 6-8 people.

FRENCH FRIED ONION RINGS, CAULIFLOWER
OR MUSHROOMS

These are really good, allow 1/2 onion per person.

Slice onions into rings and separate to dry. Coat with flour.

Make a thin fritter batter of:

Blend in a bowl and set aside:

1 1/2 c. flour
1/2 tsp. salt
1 1/2 tsp. baking powder

Mix together:

2 eggs
1 1/4 c. milk
1/4 c. vegetable oil

Beat until smooth with flour mixture.

Fry onions at 375 degrees until golden brown. Grease should be only 1 inch deep in pan, just enough to float food.

When grease is hot, 375 degrees, dip dry onions into fritter batter and let excess drip off. Fry until golden brown. Remove and place on a plate that is piled with paper towel to soak up excess grease.

FRENCH TOAST STICKS

2 eggs
1 c. milk
1 tbsp. butter
4 slices bread, cut into 4 pieces lengthwise
Sugar
Cinnamon
Maple syrup

Melt butter. Mix eggs, milk and vanilla in bowl. Beat well, soak slices of bread. Brown bread in frying pan. Sprinkle with sugar and cinnamon and serve with maple syrup.

FRIED MOZZARELLA STICKS

1 lb. Mozzarella
3 eggs
1 c. seasoned bread crumbs
Light vegetable oil

Cut cheese into 2 inch long, 1/2 inch wide sticks. Dip cheese into beaten eggs and then into bread crumbs two times. Freeze for about 10 minutes (can be overnight). Fry until golden brown (about 2 minutes on each side).

GOURMET CHICKEN ENCHILADAS

4 large chicken breasts
1 large onion chopped finely
10 large flour tortillas (or use low carb wheat tortillas)
2 T butter
1 can rotel diced tomatoes
1/4 cup sliced jalapeneos
3 cups shredded Colby Jack cheese
1 8 oz. brick cream cheese softened
1 pint sour cream
2 T chopped cilantro
1 tsp Cavenders greek seasoning
1/2 tsp garlic powder
1/2 tsp chili powder
1 pkg cream of chicken Cup-o-Soup

Boil chicken in lightly salted water until tender. Dice and set aside.

In large saucepan, saute onions until tender. Stir in Rotel, diced chicken, 1 cup Colby Jack cheese, cream cheese, 1 cup of the sour cream, 1 T cilantro, Cavenders, and garlic powder.

Taste the mixture and add more seasonings, if needed.

Grease large casserole dish and preheat oven to 375 degrees.

Fill each tortilla with 1 cup chicken mixture and roll up. Lay filled tortillas into casserole with seams on the bottom.

In medium size mixing bowl, whisk together the other cup of sour cream, the dry Cup-o-Soup contents, chili powder, and 1 cup hot tap water until smooth and creamy.

Pour soup mixture over tortillas. Sprinkle with 2 cups Colby Jack cheese, and the other T of cilantro. Lay jalapenos on top if desired.

Bake uncovered for 30 minutes until cheese is melted and slightly browned. Allow to cool for 5 minutes before serving.

GREEN BEAN, DILL AND BLUE CHEESE SALAD

DILL SEED DRESSING:

1 c. oil
1/4 c. vinegar
3 tbsp. lemon juice
1/4 tsp. pepper
1/4 tsp. paprika
1/2 tsp. dry mustard
1 to 2 cloves garlic, minced
1 tbsp. dill seed or dill weed

Mix all dressing ingredients together and refrigerate.

SALAD:

2 lb. fresh green beans, clean and break into pieces
1 bunch green onions, chopped
1/2 lb. bacon
1/4 lb. Blue cheese, to garnish
1/4 c. mayonnaise
2 tbsp. sour cream

Steam beans al dente. Drain and set aside. Fry bacon until crisp; drain and crumble. Reserve 1 tablespoon bacon for later. When ready to mix salad, mix only 1/4 cup of dressing with mayonnaise and sour cream. Mix well and pour over beans, onions and bacon. Top with Blue cheese and reserved bacon.

GRILLED QUESADILLAS

for 1 quesadilla:
2 tortillas
1/4 c. sliced olives
1/4 c. chopped chicken, pork etc.
1/2 c. shredded cheese
small amount chopped dry onion and green peppers,(hot peppers can be used if desired)
spicy tomato sauce
multiply above ingtedients to make more than one.

Chop and mix filling ingredients together.

Preheat electric grill.

Butter one side of each tortilla.

When grill is hot, lay one tortilla on grill, buttered side down. Spread filling across the tortilla and cover with the other pre-greased tortilla---buttered side up.

Lower the lid of the grill and cook until tortillas have browned and cheese has melted. About 5 minutes.

GRILL ROASTED GREEN CHILES STUFFED
WITH GUACAMOLE

8 Anaheim or long green chiles
olive oil
4 ripe haas avocados
4 ripe medium tomatoes, halved, seeded, and coarsely chopped
1 small onion, finely chopped
2 cloves garlic, minced
3 small scallions (white and green parts), finely chopped
3/4 cup chopped fresh cilantro
3 tablespoons lime juice
1 small jalapeno, seeded and finely chopped
kosher salt and freshly ground black pepper

Grill the chiles: Heat the grill or broiler. Lightly brush the chiles with oil, grill on high heat until very blackened and blistered, turning frequently, about 15 minutes. Seal the chiles in a paper bag, or foil, and allow them to steam 10 minutes. Peel away the skin being careful not to rip off the stem.

With a paring knife, make a vertical slit from the top of each chile to about 1/2 inch from the tail and remove the seeds. Be sure to leave the ribs in, or the flesh will come with them.

Prepare the guacamole:

Peel and pit the avocados and put the flesh in a large bowl. Add the tomatoes, onion, garlic, scallions, lime juice and jalapeno; mash with fork until blended but still fairly chunky.

Season to taste with salt and pepper.

Spoon the guacamole into the chiles. Serve chilled or at cool room temperature.

GUACAMOLE

Avocado Salad:

1 ripe tomato, peeled
2 avocados
1/2 onion, minced
1 tablespoon vinegar
1 chopped green chile, or to taste
salt and pepper to taste

Mash together the tomato and avocados. Stir in remaining ingredients.

Serve with warm tortillas.

Optional: Mix in pomegranate seeds for added color and a unique but authentic variation.

GUACAMOLE BEAN CASSEROLE DIP

1 can refried beans (spicy if desired)
1 can green chiles, chopped
1 1/2 c. guacamole, chilled
1 jar Ortega green chili salsa
Grated Cheddar cheese (Optional: Mozzarella cheese mixed with Cheddar)

Heat in small saucepan: beans and 1/2 can of green chiles. Layer in pan or casserole dish: beans, guacamole, salsa, chiles, and top with cheese.

HOT APPETIZERS

1 c. Hellmann's
2 c. grated Cheddar cheese
1 c. ripe olives, chopped
2 tbsp. chopped onion
1/2 c. crisp bacon
1/4 c. green pepper

Spread on party rye bread. Bake at 350 degrees for 15 minutes. Make ahead of time and freeze. Makes about 30. Delicious.

HOT CRABMEAT APPETIZER

1 (8 oz.) pkg. cream cheese
1 (6 1/2 oz.) can crabmeat, flaked
2 tbsp. finely chopped onion
1 tbsp. milk
1/2 tsp. creamy horseradish
1/4 tsp. salt
Dash of pepper
1/3 c. sliced almonds, toasted

Combine all ingredients except almonds, mixing until well blended. Sprinkle with almonds. Bake 15 minutes at 375 degrees. Serve hot with cold crisp pieces of raw vegetables. Especially good with crisp cold cauliflower.

HOT MEXICAN BEAN DIP

1 8 oz. pkg Philly Cream Cheese, softened
1 cup sour cream
1 can refried beans
1 tablespoon garlic, finely minced
1 tablespoon cilantro, chopped
2 tablespoon Lipton's onion soup mix
2 tablespoons chili powder
2 1/2 cups grated cheddar or Monterey Jack cheese
2 tablespoons chili powder
pinch of salt
1 tablespoon Tabasco (green) pepper sauce

Soak the minced garlic in the hot pepper sauce for 10 minutes. If you don't have green pepper sauce, you can substitute red Tabasco.

Combine cream cheese, sour cream, beans, cilantro, onion soup mix and chili powder and a pinch of salt to taste. Stir in garlic and Tabasco sauce when ready.

Top with cheese.

Garnish with chopped cilantro and a sprinkle of chili powder, paprika, parsley, or a dollop of sour cream.

KIDS PIZZA SNACK

2 English muffins
1/4 c. Ragu sauce
Slices of cheese

Open muffins. Toast lightly in oven. Leave oven on. Spread Ragu on each 1/2. Cover with slices of cheese. Toast in oven until cheese bubbles.

LAYERED CRAB MOLD

4 (8 oz.) pkg. softened cream cheese
1/2 c. mayonnaise
2 tbsp. lemon juice
2 tbsp. grated onion
2 tbsp. Worcestershire sauce
1/8 tsp. garlic powder
2 (7 1/2 oz.) cans well drained crab meat
2 (12 oz.) bottles chili sauce
1 c. chopped parsley

Grease 8 inch springform mold. Mix first 6 ingredients until well blended. Spread on bottom of springform mold.

Spread crab meat over cheese layer. Spread chili sauce over crab meat layer. Cover with Saran or foil. Refrigerate overnight. Remove sides and sprinkle with parsley. Serve with crackers. Serves 20.

LAYERED MEXICAN DIP

1 can refried beans
1 container sour cream
1 lb ground beef
1 packet taco seasoning
1 pouch shredded taco cheese
1 container salsa

Brown beef and add taco seasoning. One thin layer at a time, alternate between the ingredients in an ovenproof round casserole, preferably clear glass. The last layer should be cheese.

Cover loosely and bake at 350* for 35 minutes, uncover and bake 10-15 more minutes or until bubbly and golden brown on top!

Serve with white corn chips.

LIL SMOKIES

1 lb. pkg. little smokie sausages
1 bottle BBQ sauce

In saucepan or crock pot put sausages and cover with BBQ sauce. Heat thru.

MACARONI AND CHEESE GARDEN SALAD

8 oz. elbow macaroni or bow-tie pasta
1 tbsp. salad oil
1 med. onion, finely chopped
1 tsp. dry mustard
12 cherry tomatoes, halved
6 oz. cheese: Smoked Mozzarella, Cheddar, and or Fontina, cut into thin
strips (1 1/2 c.)
1/4 c. coarsely chopped fresh parsley
2 tbsp. milk
1 tsp. salt
1/8 tsp. black pepper

If your kids like macaroni and cheese, they will love this salad. Use the cheeses listed or any combination you choose. Cook macaroni according to package directions. Meanwhile, heat oil in small skillet over medium heat. Add onion. Saute for 5 minutes or until golden brown, stirring frequently. Add mustard; cook, stirring for 1 minute. Remove onion mixture to large serving container.

Drain macaroni and rinse with cold water; drain again. Add to onion mixture with tomatoes, cheeses, and parsley. In a small bowl, mix mayonnaise, milk, salt, and pepper until smooth. Pour over macaroni mixture; toss until well coated. Cover and refrigerate. (Salad will absorb dressing and if necessary, stir in a little milk before serving.) Makes 6 servings.

MARINATED BEEF STRIPS

1 lb. cooked roast beef
1 sm. onion, sliced
3/4 tsp. salt
Pepper to taste
1 1/2 tbsp. lemon juice
1 c. dairy sour cream

Cut meat in thin strips. Separate onion into rings. Combine beef, onion, salt and pepper. Sprinkle with lemon juice. Stir in sour cream. Chill. Serve in lettuce lined dishes. Serves 6.

MARINATED MUSHROOMS

Combine in a glass or stoneware bowl:

1 lb mushrooms, cleaned
1 tablespoon chopped chives or scallions

In a small bowl, combine:

2 tablespoons red wine vinegar or cider vinegar
5 tablespoons extra virgin olive oil
1 teaspoon Creole or coarse German mustard
1/2 teaspoon salt
4-5 drops of Tabasco
1 tablespoon fresh basil, minced
1 teaspoon dried parsley
1/2 teaspoon dried oregano
2 cloves garlic, pressed
pinch red pepper flakes

Whisk together ingredients for dressing; pour over the mushrooms and marinate for one hour, turning occasionally.

Serve at room temperature. Keeps well in refrigerator.

NACHO CASSEROLE

2 cans refried beans
1 lb. ground meat
1 onion, chopped
1 can chopped green chilies
3 c. grated Monterey Jack cheese
1 sm. jar taco sauce
1 sm. carton sour cream
1 pkg. Avocado Dip (found in frozen foods section)
Ripe olives, sliced

Spread beans on bottom of well-greased 3 quart casserole (Corningware works well). Saute meat with onion, drain and spread over beans. Cover with chilies, grated cheese and taco sauce. Bake at 400 degrees for 20 to 25 minutes. Spread sour cream down middle and top with avocado dip and ripe olives. Swirl dip, sour cream and olives to mix. Serve with nacho chips or Doritos.

NACHO CHEESE SAUCE

1/4 c. chopped green pepper
1/4 c. chopped red pepper
4 to 5 cloves garlic, minced
2 scallions, minced
1 tbsp. olive oil
2 tbsp. butter
2 tbsp. flour
1 1/2 cups milk
1 c. cheddar cheese, shredded
1/4 teaspoon Tabasco sauce
2 tbsp. minced jalapeno peppers
1/4 teaspoon salt
Pinch cayenne pepper
1/4 teaspoon paprika
nacho corn chips

Mix together peppers, olive oil, garlic and butter in a saucepan.

Sprinkle in flour, pour in milk and stir until mixture simmers -- do not allow to boil. When mixture begins to thicken, stir in the cheese and remaining ingredients, Simmer on low heat an additional five minutes or until cheese is fully melted.

Serve with nacho chips.

NACHO DIP

1 1/2 lb. hamburger, fried
1 pkg. taco seasoning
1 can refried beans
Nacho cheese
1 jar Chi-Chis Picante sauce, mild

Fry hamburger; drain grease. Add taco seasoning and Picante sauce. Layer refried beans on bottom of baking dish. Then spread hamburger mixture over beans. Then sprinkle cheese over hamburger. Heat in a 350 degree oven until warm through. Use as a dip for Doritos or Tostitos.

OYSTERS ROCKEFELLER

2 doz. oysters
Shallots
Parsley
butter
Drained, cooked spinach
Lettuce
See options below
Ground anise seed
Lemon juice
Lea and Perrins
Plain bread crumbs
Parmesan cheese
Oyster liquid

Drain oysters, reserve liquid. Put shallots and parsley in a glass measuring cup covered with butter. Cover cup and microwave for 2 minutes, stirring halfway through. Put this in blender with spinach, celery, lettuce, oyster liquid, anise seeds, lemon juice and Lea and Perrin. Blend until smooth. Add bread crumbs to thicken (this topping can now be refrigerated for 1 week).

Place oysters on shells and shells on rock salt. Broil only until oyster edges curl. Top with sauce and broil until golden brown. (Sprinkle with Parmesan cheese before second broil.) Serve!

White wine to saute instead of butter, or bacon drippings or butter. Dijon mustard, garlic, anchovies or paste, Beau Monde or thyme can be used.

PARTY APPETIZER PIE

1 (8 oz.) pkg. cream cheese, softened
1 (2 1/2 oz.) jar dried beef, finely chopped (or substitute 5 slices bacon,
cooked crisp)
2 tbsp. finely chopped green pepper
1/2 c. sour cream
2 tbsp. milk
2 tbsp. instant onion
1/8 tsp. pepper
1/4 c. chopped nuts

Blend cream cheese and milk in a 1 quart mixing bowl. Add dried beef, onion, and green pepper. Mix well. Stir in sour cream. Spread evenly in 8 inch pie plate. Cover with waxed paper. Cook 2 minutes. 15 seconds on high or until mixture is hot. Let stand 2 minutes to firm slightly. Sprinkle with nuts; garnish with parsley. Serve with assorted crackers.

PARTY CREAM CHEESE PINWHEELS

10 large flour tortillas
2 boxes of cream cheese
1 cup pitted black olives, finely chopped
2 tablespoons pimentos, finely chopped
1 pkg ranch dressing
2 tablespoons green jalapenos, finely chopped

Soften cream cheese Mix in the powdered Ranch dressing Add the pimentos, black olives and the jalapenos.

Spread evenly over the flour tortillas using a rubber spatula. Roll tightly. Cover and chill for about one hour. Slice into pinwheels.

PASTA AND MOZZARELLA SALAD

8 oz. corkscrew macaroni
1 recipe Parmesan dressing
10 oz. fresh spinach, torn
8 oz. cubed Mozzarella cheese
8 oz. thinly sliced ham or mold pepperham
1 (4 oz.) can green chili peppers, drained

Cook macaroni. Drain. Toss with dressing; add remaining ingredients. Cover, chill. Sprinkle 2 tablespoon grated Parmesan over each serving (6 to 8 servings)

PARMESAN DRESSING:

Place 1 egg in blender, blend 5 seconds. With blender running, slowly add 1 cup salad oil until thick. Add 1/2 cup Parmesan, 1/4 cup white wine vinegar, 1/2 to 1 tsp. pepper, 1/2 teaspoon salt, 1/4 teaspoon ground cloves, 1 to 2 cloves garlic, minced. Blend until smooth.

PASTA SALAD

2 c. fresh snow peas
2 c. broccoli florettes
2 c. fresh mushrooms
2 1/2 c. cherry tomato halves
1 can black olives, sliced & drained
1 (8 oz.) pkg. cheese stuffed tortellini
1 (8 oz.) pkg. fettucini, broken
1 tbsp. Parmesan

Mix vegetables together. Cook pastas according to package directions; cool. Combine with vegetables. Add dressing; toss well. Chill several hours before serving. Garnish with extra Parmesan. This makes a BIG salad.

DRESSING:

1/2 tsp. each pepper, sugar & oregano
1 tsp. each dried dillweed & salt
1 1/2 tsp. Dijon mustard
2 tsp. dried whole basil
2 tbsp. chopped fresh parsley
2 cloves garlic, minced
1/2 c. sliced green onion
1/3 c. each vegetable oil, olive oil & red wine vinegar

Combine all ingredients in a jar; shake well. Pour over salad. Serves 10 to 12.

PEA, CHEESE AND PICKLE SALAD

1 lg. can green peas, drained
1 sm. jar sweet gherkin pickles
6 oz. Cheddar cheese
Mayonnaise to mix salad

Drain peas, slice pickles and cube cheese. Mix with enough mayonnaise to blend salad. Chill.

PEANUT BUTTER MARSHMALLOW PINWHEELS

3 cups sugar
1/2 cup light Karo syrup
1/2 cup hot water
2 egg whites, beaten until stiff
1/4 tsp. vanilla
peanut butter - 1 jar (maybe less - it depends on how much you like peanut butter)
I love this recipe. I used to buy candy like this in Kentucky gift shops. It is great, but hard to get right.

Cook sugar, Karo syrup and water in medium sized boiling pan on medium-high until mixture begins to form small balls. When you pull out the spoon, the mixture is very stringy. Remove from heat.

While mixture above is cooking, begin beating 2 egg whites and 1/4 tsp. vanilla in a large bowl with mixer until stiff peaks appear. Let set until sugar mixture is ready.

Begin pouring sugar mixture into egg whites very slowly as you continue to beat with the mixer. Once all of the sugar mixture is added, turn off the mixer and stir by hand. Continue stirring the mixture until it is very hard to move by hand, don't let the mixture get too hard. The mixture should be a little soft (marshmallow like) and a little sticky.

Pour the mixture onto a table coated with butter and a small dusting of powdered sugar. Quickly pat out the mixture and lightly spread it out like biscuit dough with a roller. Don't roll it too thin. Quickly spread peanut butter all over mixture. Roll up log quickly, might still be a little sticky, just pat the log with powdered sugar as you roll it up.

Let the log sit and cool down to room temperature, then cut into pinwheel slices.

PELLMINI

Dough:

1 cup milk
1 tablespoon salt
5 eggs
1 tablespoon sour cream or buttermilk (if available)
flour, enough to make a soft dough

Filling:

1 lb. chopped tri-tip steak or ground beef
1 lb. ground pork
2 onions, finely chopped
4 cloves garlic, minced
1 stalk celery, finely chopped
1/4 cup fresh parsley, minced
1 tablespoon each butter and olive oil
salt and pepper to taste

Beat together eggs, salt and milk. If you have sour cream or buttermilk available, add 1 tablespoon to make a more tender and tasty dough.

Stir in enough flour to make a dough which is soft but can be rolled out. Let rest a few minutes. Knead dough until smooth.

Saute the meat, onions, garlic, and celery in butter and oil, adding the parsley at the last minute. Drain excess liquid and allow to cool.

Roll out dough and cut into circles. Fill centers, each with 1 tablespoon of meat mixture. Fold sides together (like a clam shell) and pinch the edges together firmly. You can freeze these at this point by placing on a cookie sheet in the freezer. Remove from cookie sheet 1 hour later (or when frozen solid) and drop into ziploc bags, ready to serve when needed.

To serve, boil 6-7 minutes in chicken, beef, or ham broth. (Very good in the leftover broth from a boiled ham!). They will rise to the surface when cooked.

Serve with a dollop of sour cream or with melted butter.

Can also saute in melted butter with onions or leeks.

PEPPERONI PINWHEELS

3-4 fajita sized flour tortillas
10 slices pepperoni
2 t. Kraft Shredded Parmesan, Romano, and Asiago (in dairy section)
4 oz softened cream cheese
1/8 t. dried minced onions
1/16 t. garlic salt
dash or 2 of pepper
¼ t. freeze-dried or fresh chives
dash chili powder
¼ t. parsley flakes
smidgen dill weed
smidgen oregano
dash hidden valley ranch seasoning

Dice up pepperoni. Mix all ingredients except flour tortillas in a small bowl. Stir together well. Spread onto flour shells. Roll up then put in refrigerator or freezer until cream cheese is firm. Slice up into desired pieces.

PINEAPPLE CHEESE SALAD

1 sm. can crushed pineapple, drained
1 (3 oz.) pkg. cream cheese
1/2 c. salad dressing
4 c. miniature marshmallows
1 c. whipping cream
1/8 tsp. salt

Cream together cream cheese and salad dressing. Add pineapple and marshmallows. Whip cream, add salt and fold into first mixture. Pour into a greased mold and refrigerate. Green grapes may be added.

PIZZA SNACKS

Favorite pizza flavors top crackers for a crunchy appetizer.

1 c. finely chopped turkey ham
1 c. (4 oz.) shredded Mozzarella cheese
1 stalk celery, diced fine
1/4 c. sliced pimento-stuffed olives
2 tbsp. mayonnaise or salad dressing
1/2 tsp. Italian seasoning
About 60 unsalted wheat crackers

Combine all ingredients except crackers in 1-quart microwave-safe bowl; mix well. Arrange crackers on 3 microwave-safe serving plates. Spoon a teaspoonful of mixture onto each cracker.

Microwave (high) one plate at a time, uncovered, 45 to 60 minutes or until cheese starts to melt, rotating plate once. Serve warm.

To finely chop ham, remove outer layer and process in food processor.

Pizza Snacks can be assembled several hours ahead and heated just before servings.

POPCORN CHICKEN

4 chicken breasts
1-2 tbs cajun powder
basmati rice
1/2 cup vegetable oil

Batter chicken breats with a cooks knife and cut up into tiny bits, roughly. Put into a frying pan with the oil and stir over medium heat.

Before the chicken has whitened shake on Cajun powder to taste.

Leave cooking until well done & crispy black (looks burnt but tastes perfect).

Serve on a bed of Basmati rice with garnishes.

QUICK PAN NACHOS

1 large can refried beans
1 lb hamburger
1 package taco seasoning
3-4 cups grated cheddar cheese
1 medium can sliced olives
1 large or 2 med chopped tomatoes
1 bunch green onions chopped
sour cream
guacamole
salsa

Brown hamburger and add taco seasoning as package instructs. While hamburger simmers, spread the refried beans into the bottom of the baking dish and place in the oven under the broiler until beans are hot all the way through.

Top beans with hamburger mixture and then spread cheese evenly over the top.

Place back under the broiler until cheese is melted. Top with green onions, tomatoes and olives.

Cut into wedges and spoon onto a plate, top with sour cream, guacamole and salsa then surround with corn chips.

Scoop up with the chips and enjoy!

ROTEL (CON QUESO) DIP

1 to 2 cans Ro-Tel tomatoes with chilies
2 lb. Velveeta cheese

Melt Velveeta over low heat; mix in tomatoes until warm. Enjoy as a dip for tortilla chips. Also if you are on a budget, 2 cans of Cheddar cheese soup can substitute for Velveeta.

SAUSAGE BALLS

1 lb. hot sausage
1 lb. mild sausage
12 oz. sharp cheese (softened)
12 oz. mellow cheese (softened)
4 cups Bisquick

Mix all ingredients. Roll into small balls. Place on cookie sheets.

Bake at 400 for 10-15 minutes, or until done (depends upon the size).

Best served warm.

SHRIMP AND CRAB COCKTAIL

1 can med. to lg. shrimp, cleaned
1 can crab, cleaned
1 bottle cocktail sauce
1 tbsp. lemon juice
1 tbsp. horseradish
1 tbsp. Worcestershire sauce

Mix cocktail sauce, lemon juice, horseradish, and Worcestershire sauce, add shrimp and crab. Refrigerate overnight before serving. Very spicy.

SHRIMP AND SCALLOP SCAMPI OVER
LINGUINI

2 lbs. fresh, peeled and deveined, cooked shrimp
1 1/2 lbs. sm. bay scallops
2 lbs. linguini pasta, cooked and drained
8 tbsp. butter
1 med. onion, chopped
1 tbsp. minced garlic
1 tsp. chopped parsley
1 tsp. crushed red pepper (more or less to taste)
Grated Parmesan or Romano cheese

Cook and drain linguini. Keep warm. Melt butter in large no-stick fry or saucepan. Add onion, saute for about 3 minutes. Add garlic, parsley and crushed red pepper, stir and add scallops, stirring constantly for 3 minutes until scallops are done (will turn from opaque to white).

SHRIMP COCKTAIL

2 c. lettuce, shredded
1 lb. boiled shrimp, peeled & chilled
3/4 c. Zippy Cocktail Sauce
Lemon wedges

Arrange lettuce on individual serving plates. Top with chilled boiled shrimp; drizzle with Zippy Cocktail Sauce before serving. Garnish with lemon wedges. 4 to 6 appetizer servings.

ZIPPY COCKTAIL SAUCE:

2/3 c. chili sauce
1/4 c. lemon juice
2 to 3 tbsp. prepared horseradish
2 tsp. Worcestershire sauce
1/4 tsp. hot sauce

Combine all ingredients, stirring until smooth. Cover and chill at least 2 hours. Yield: 1 cup.

SHRIMP MOLD

1 c. chili sauce
1 tbsp. lemon juice
1 lg. pkg. cream cheese
2 tbsp. gelatin
1/2 c. mayonnaise
1/4 c. chopped celery
1/4 c. chopped onion
1/4 c. chopped green pepper
1 lg. can drained shrimp

Heat chili sauce and lemon juice. Add gelatin, dissolved in 1/4 cup water and cream cheese. Beat well. Add other ingredients and pour into mold.

SOUTHERN EGG ROLL

1 lb. pork butt
1 bottle of your favorite bbq sauce
1/3 white vinegar
salt
pepper
cole slaw (premade or home made, whichever you prefer)
egg roll sheets
eggs
milk

Preheat oven to 300°F.

THE MEAT Take the pork and cute it into 4 equal size blocks. Season pork with salt and pepper. Place in baking dish and pour in vinegar and BBQ sauce so that it coats the meat.

Place pork covered in oven for 3 hours. DO NOT UNCOVER OR CHECK THE MEAT UNTIL THE TIME IS UP!! Take out and check to see if meat "pulls" easily, if not cook another 30 minutes. Pull pork and place in a bowl.

Preheat deep fryer to 350°F.

Take 2 eggs and mix with 2 teaspoons of milk; whisk together.

Take one egg roll, lay out and place some meat and slaw on the inside. Roll up the wrap very tightly, but do not let the roll rip.

Use the egg to hold together the wrap as though you are sealing an envelope.

Repeat for as many as you want to make. Dip entire roll in the egg; shake off and put in deep fryer.

Deep fry for 2-3 min until they are golden brown. Take out and place on paper towel.

You can eat these just like this or make a Tabasco mayo.

Just mix some milk Tabasco and mayonnaise together to make a dressing consistency.

SPICY DEVILLED EGGS

6 hard cooked eggs
1 tbsp. fresh parsley
1 tbsp. scallions, minced
1 small jalapeno pepper
1/4 cup Miracle Whip
1/4 cup shredded cheddar cheese
1 tsp. Dijon mustard
1/2 teaspoon cilantro (optional)
pinch cayenne pepper
pinch chili powder
1/4 teaspoon salt
1/2 teaspoon paprika
1/2 teaspoon horseradish, grated
1/4 teaspoon celery seed

Slice each egg in half crosswise. Scrape out yolks saving contents in a bowl. Add mayonnaise, mustard and blend together. Add remaining ingredients to combine.

Spoon approximately 1 tbsp. of the yolk mixture into each egg half. Sprinkle lightly with chili powder and paprika. Garnish with a sprig of parsley.

SPINACH APPETIZER

1 pkg. frozen chopped spinach, cooked, drained and cooled
1 (8 oz.) pkg. softened cream cheese
1/2 c. mayonnaise
1/3 c. Parmesan cheese
6 slices crisp crumbled bacon
Garlic powder to taste
flour tortillas

Blend all ingredients well. Spread on tortilla shells. Roll up and chill. Slice about 1/2 inch thick. Serve.

STUFFED MUSHROOM

1/2 medium onion, minced
1 shallot, chopped (optional)
mushroom stems, chopped
mushroom caps (for stuffing)
onion and garlic powder
paprika
breadcrumbs
2 tablespoons freshly chopped parsley (optional)
butter

Choose mushrooms with large caps. Brush mushrooms cleaning well. Remove caps from stems, reserving caps. Melt butter in sauté pan and add mushroom stems, onion, shallots, if using. Sauté until onions are transparent.

Remove from heat and stir together bread crumbs, onion and garlic powder and parsley. Add enough breadcrumb mixture so that mixture is no longer soupy. Stuff mushrooms caps and sprinkle pressed-in stuffing with paprika.

SWEDISH MEATBALLS

Meatballs:

2 lbs ground chuck
1 1/2 teaspoon garlic powder
1 teaspoon seasoning salt
1/2 teaspoon pepper
1/4 cup plain bread crumbs

Sauce:

1 bottle chili sauce
1 jar grape jelly

Preheat oven to 350°F. Combine garlic powder, seasoning salt, pepper and bread crumbs with ground chuck. Mix well and make into meatballs. Cook in preheated oven 30-35 mins or until done.

While meatballs are baking, combine 1 bottle of chili sauce and grape jelly in a saucepan and heat until jelly has melted.

When meatballs are done, remove from oven. Drain and transfer meatballs to saucepan and coat well with sauce before serving.

SWEET AND SOUR MEAT BALLS

1 1/2 c. chicken bouillon
1 green pepper, chunked
6 slices pineapple chunks
2 tbsp. soy sauce
3/4 c. vinegar
3/4 c. pineapple juice
3/4 c. sugar
Salt and pepper to taste

Thicken with 2 tablespoons cornstarch.

MEAT BALLS:

1 1/2 lbs. ground round
2 eggs
Bread crumbs to thicken

TACO CASSEROLE

1 lb. ground beef
1 med. onion, chopped (1/2 c.)
1 (8 oz.) can tomato sauce
1/4 c. water
1 tsp. chili powder
1 (16 oz.) can refried beans
1/4 c. taco sauce
1 1/2 c. shredded Monterey Jack cheese (6 oz.)
5 taco or tostado shells, coarsely crushed
1 c. shredded lettuce
1 sm. tomato, chopped (1/4 c.) (optional)
1/4 c. sliced green onion (optional)
1/4 c. sliced pitted ripe olives (optional)
1 (6 oz.) container frozen avocado dip (optional)

Crumble the beef into a 1 1/2 quart casserole, then stir in onion. Micro-cook, covered, on 100% power (HIGH) 4 1/2 to 5 1/2 minutes or until done. Drain, then stir in tomato sauce, water and chili powder. Micro-cook, covered, on 100% power (HIGH) about 6 minutes or until bubbly.

Meanwhile, stir together beans and tomato sauce. Spread in bottom of a 12 x 7 1/2 x 2 inch baking dish, then spread the meat mixture atop. Micro-cook, uncovered, on 100% power (HIGH) 7 to 9 minutes or until heated through.

Top with cheese. Micro-cook, uncovered, on 100% power (HIGH) about 1 minute or until cheese is melted.

Top with crushed taco or tostado shells and lettuce. If desired, top with tomato, green onion, olives and avocado dip. Makes 6 servings.

TACO DIP

1 can refried beans
1 packet taco seasoning
1/2 cup mayonnaise
1 cup sour cream
shredded cheddar cheese
chopped tomatoes
sliced black olives

Spread refried beans on bottom of dish. Mix mayonnaise, sour cream and taco seasoning. Layer mixture on top of beans. Top with shredded cheese, olives, and tomatoes. Serve with tortilla chips.

Optional toppings: onions, jalapenos, etc.

This is a super easy recipe that I've made over and over for different gatherings. I actually get requests for it now and there's never any leftovers!

TACO-SEASONED CHEX MIX

Tex-Mex meets Chex in this easy snackin' mix made with taco seasoning mix – yum!

3 cups Corn Chex cereal
2 cups bite-size cheese crackers
2 cups bite-size pretzel twists
1 cup salted peanuts
3 tablespoons vegetable oil
2 tablespoons water
1 package (1.25 oz) Old El Paso taco seasoning mix

In large microwavable bowl, mix cereals, crackers, pretzels and peanuts.

In small bowl, stir together oil, water and taco seasoning mix. Pour over cereal mixture, stirring until evenly coated.

 Microwave uncovered on High about 5 minutes, stirring every 2 minutes, until mixture begins to brown. Spread on waxed paper or foil to cool, about 15 minutes. Store in airtight container.

THREE CHEESE DIP

1/2 c. crumbled Blue cheese
1/2 shredded sharp natural Cheddar cheese
1/2 c. cottage cheese
1/4 c. dairy sour cream
1 1/2 tsp. grated onions
1/2 tsp. Worcestershire sauce

Combine cheeses and let come to room temperature. Beat with electric mixer until smooth and creamy. Add remaining ingredients; beat until fluffy. Chill. Serve with crackers or chips. Makes 1 1/2 cups.

TUNA MOLD

2 (6 1/2 oz.) cans tuna, drained
1/2 tsp. Tabasco sauce
1 tsp. instant dried minced onion
1 (8 oz.) soft cream cheese
2 tbsp. chili sauce
2 tbsp. chopped dried parsley

Mix all ingredients with mixer. Pour into "Pammed" mold or form into ball and refrigerate 3 hours. Serve with Party Pumpernickel Bread, Party Rye or your favorite crackers.

WHEAT FLOUR TORTILLA

1/2 c. all-purpose flour
1/2 c. whole wheat flour
1/4 tsp. salt
1 tbsp. vegetable oil
6 tbsp. water

Mix all ingredients together. Form in a ball; divide into 9 pieces on a lightly floured board, roll out. Cut each in a circle, using a saucer as a guide.

Heat a large ungreased frying pan. Cook each tortilla without overlapping, until dry, turn once. Use immediately for enchiladas or for tacos, bend into a taco shape. Makes 9.